Welcome aboard!

This year, you are going on an amazing handwriting journey to a world of joins and links. Be sure to have your passport ready.

Handwriting Passport

Name: ____________________

Age: ____________________

Five things about me:

1 ____________________

2 ____________________

3 ____________________

4 ____________________

5 ____________________

Review: Lower-case anticlockwise printing

Trace then copy.

Remember to sit the letters on the main line correctly.

u y v

w a g

q c o

s d e

Make up your own patterns using these letter shapes.

Handwriting: anticlockwise fluency patterns, lower-case printing revision.

Trace then copy.

Make up your own patterns using these letter shapes.

Handwriting: clockwise fluency patterns, lower-case printing revision.

Review: Lower-case downstroke printing

Trace then copy.

Remember to keep the slope the same.

l t
i j
f x
z

Make up your own patterns using these letter shapes.

Handwriting: downstroke fluency patterns, lower-case printing revision.

Make the letters stretch and shrink.

Handwriting: forming letters correctly, keeping slope consistent. **Literary elements:** reference to characters from *Alice's Adventures in Wonderland* by Lewis Carroll (1865).

Use these words to label the robot. Use your best printing.

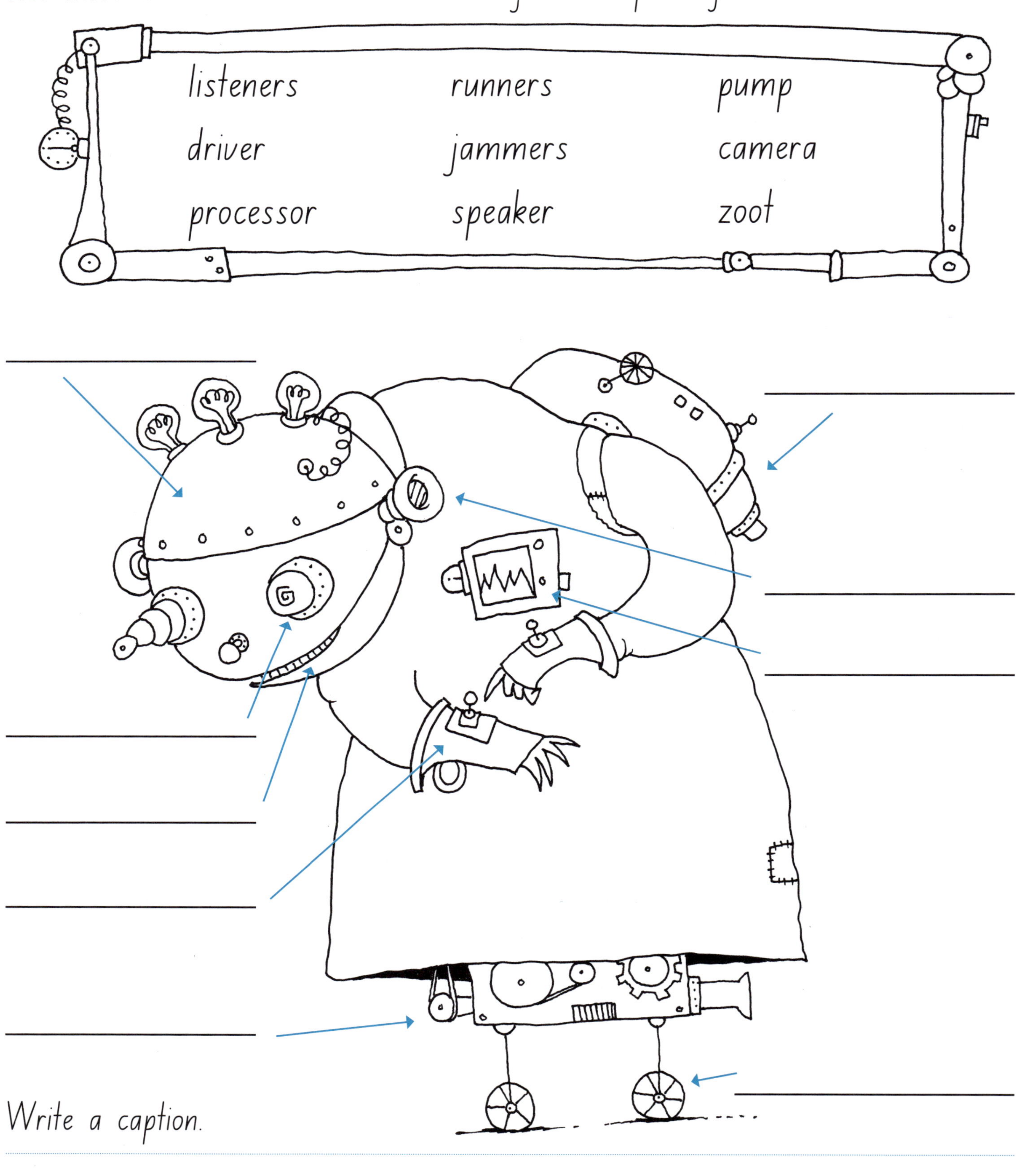

Write a caption.

Handwriting: using printing to label diagrams. **Spelling and vocabulary:** technical words. **Literary elements:** science fiction genre.

Capital letters always sit on the main line.

Trace then write the capitals that use downstrokes.

A E F H

I J K L

M N T V

W X Y Z

Trace then write the capitals that use anticlockwise movements.

C G O Q

S U

Trace then write the capitals that use clockwise movements.

B D P R

Write the missing capital letters.

A __ C D __ __ G H __ __

__ L __ N __ P __ R S __

__ V __ __ __ Z

Handwriting: capital letters revision, capitals always sit on the main ine. **Spelling:** alphabetical order.

Use this spelling alphabet when you want to be clearly understood.

Trace the NATO alphabet.

Alpha Bravo Charlie
Delta Echo Foxtrot
Golf Hotel India
Juliet Kilo Lima
Mike November Oscar
Papa Quebec Romeo
Sierra Tango Uniform
Victor Whiskey X-ray
Yankee Zulu

Spell your name in the NATO alphabet.

Handwriting: lower-case and capital letters revision. **Spelling and vocabulary:** alphabetical order, codes, NATO alphabet.

Trace the capital letter and then make up your own alphabet.

A B C

D E F

G H I

J K L

M N O

P Q R

S T U

V W X

Y Z

Spell a friend's name in your new alphabet.

Handwriting: lower-case and capital letters revision. **Spelling:** alphabetical order, codes.

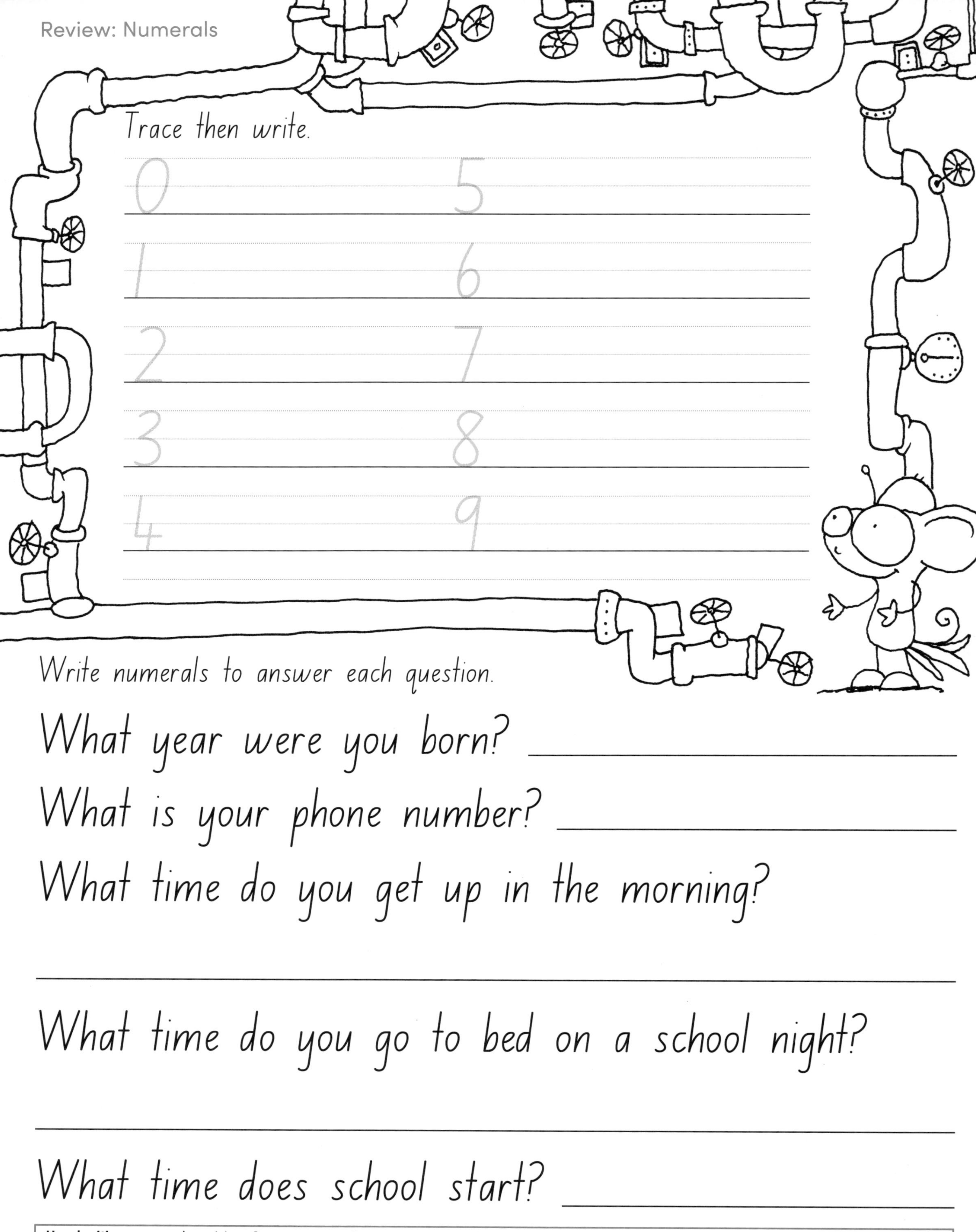

Trace then write.

0 5

1 6

2 7

3 8

4 9

Write numerals to answer each question.

What year were you born? ______________

What is your phone number? ______________

What time do you get up in the morning?

____

What time do you go to bed on a school night?

____

What time does school start? ______________

Handwriting: numerals revision. **Grammar:** questions.

Practise.

. . , , ? ? ! !

: : ; ; - - – –

' ' " " " "

Trace then write.

"What do you call a collection

of letters?" asked the teacher.

"That's the alphabet!" shouted

the class.

That elephant can spell!

e

Handwriting: punctuation revision. **Grammar:** collective noun (class), saying verbs (asked, shouted), being verbs ('is' in That's). **Punctuation:** full stop, comma, question mark, exclamation mark, colon, semi-colon, hyphen, dash, apostrophe, quotation marks. **Spelling and vocabulary:** contraction (That's).

Watch your letter size, letter shape and slope. Make sure your letters face the right way.

Rewrite the text correctly.

"WHat dO You CALL a grOUP

of chilDren?" asked SanJay.

"That's a ɔLazz!" yellEd RoSie.

"You're corrEct". saidtheTEAcher.

Self assessment

My letter shapes need to improve ☐ are good ☐ are fantastic ☐ .

My letter sizes are inconsistent ☐ are good ☐ are fantastic ☐ .

My letter slope is inconsistent ☐ is good ☐ is consistently good ☐ .

Handwriting: slope, letter shape, letter size. **Grammar:** question, exclamation, saying verbs (asked, yelled), collective noun (class), being verbs ('is' in That's , 'are' in You're. **Punctuation:** full stop, capital letter to start a sentence, exclamation mark, question mark, quotation marks. **Spelling and vocabulary:** apostrophe for contraction (That's, You're).

Letters that finish on the main line need an exit kick. This kick will help you join letters later on. Joining letters carefully helps you write faster while still making sure that others can read your writing.

Track these letters that need an exit kick.

u u u u u a a a a a

d d d d d d d m m

m m m m m n n n n

n n n n h h h h h

h h k k k k k k k

i i i i i i l l l l l l

l l l t t t t t t t t

Review: Exit kicks

Trace then write.

u

a d

m

n h

k

i l

t

Trace the letters and add exit kicks to the letters that need them.

a b c d e f g h i j k l m

n o p q r s t u v w x y z

Handwriting: quick, smooth exit kicks at the main line.

Trace then write.

hill till mill

ant land hand hind kind mind

him dim milk hut hunt mud

tilt hilt kilt lilt tan man

mint lint tint hint dint hat

Self assessment

Rate your exit kicks on a scale from 1 to 5. 1 means you need a lot more practice. 5 means your kicks are fantastic.

1 2 3 4 5

Handwriting: exit kicks at the main line. **Spelling and vocabulary**: rhyme.

Review: Exit kicks

Trace then write.

Many hands make light work.

It's raining cats and dogs.

The early bird catches the worm.

Practice makes perfect.

Handwriting: exit kicks at the main line. **Grammar:** adjectives (light, early), common nouns (hands, work, cats, dogs, bird, worm, practice). **Punctuation**: full stop, capital letter to start a sentence. **Spelling and vocabulary:** apostrophe for contraction (It's). **Literary elements**: proverbs, idiom.

Trace each word, adding exit kicks where needed. Then rewrite with all the exit kicks.

Here is the repulsant

snozzcumber!" cried the BFG,

waving it about. "I squoggle it!

I mispise it! I dispunge it!"

Make up some words of your own.

Handwriting: exit kicks at the main line. **Grammar:** statement, exc amation, adjective (repulsant), saying verb (cried), action verb (waving), thinking verbs (squoggle, mispise, dispunge), noun (snozzcumber), noun-pronoun reference (snozzcumber/it), acronym (BFG). **Punctuation**: full stop, capital letter to start a sentence, exclamation mark, comma, quotation marks. **Spelling and vocabulary**: negative prefixes mis- (in mispise for despise), dis- (in dispunge meaning to expunge or erase). **Literary elements**: quote from *The BFG* Roald Dahl (1982), neologism (snozzcumber), portmanteau word (repulsant = repulsive and unpleasant).

v and w finish at the blue line.
They have an exit hook instead of a kick.
You'll use this **hook** to hook onto the next letter when you start to join letters.

v w ← blue line
← main line

Track.

v v v v v v v v v

w w w w w w w w w

v w v w v w v w v

Trace.

v v v v v v v v v v

w w w w w w w w w

Practise.

v

w

Handwriting: exit hooks at the blue line.

Remember! These letters need an exit hook: v, w. These letters need an exit kick: a, d, h, i, k, l, m, n, t and u.

Trace then write.

v u a d w

n m h k i

l t v w k

Trace, adding the kicks or hooks where needed.

u b a c d h n m x y

m l z e h f k g i j l

w t o q r t h s p v

Trace then write.

will what wit whim win wait

van vat vault vain vim will

Handwriting: exit hooks at the blue line and exit kicks at the main line.

Trace then write.

In the sea, once

upon a time . . . there was a Whale,

and he ate fishes. He ate the

starfish and the garfish . . . and

the really truly twirly-whirly eel.

Self assessment

My exits are smooth and neat
sometimes ☐ often ☐ always ☐.

Handwriting: exit hooks at the blue line and exit kicks at the main line. **Grammar:** extended noun group for eel (article, adverbs, adjective). **Punctuation:** ellipsis to indicate words have been left out (. . .). **Spelling and vocabulary:** rhyme (twirly-whirly). **Literary elements:** quote from *Just So Stories*, 'How the Whale Got His Throat', by Rudyard Kipling (1902), common story beginning phrase 'once upon a time.'

Handwriting: entries at the blue line.

Review: Entries

Trace then write each letter.

r j p

i m u y

n v w

Circle the letters that need exit kicks. Draw a square around letters that need exit hooks. Draw a triangle around letters that need entries.

a b c d e f g h

i j k l m n o p q

r s t u v w x y z

Write some words of your own using letters that have an exit kick, an exit hook or an entry.

Which letters don't have a kick, hook or entry? List them here:

Handwriting: entries at the blue line, exit kicks and hooks.

You don't need an entry at the start of a word. Practise adding entries to letters inside words to help you join them up later.

Trace then write.

pip nip mum pup in puppy pin

jump pump rump mum mumps

jury prim primp pry wry win

Fill in the missing letters n, r, m, u.

ju_p p_ppy p_y w_y

yu_ ru_ yu_ _y ru_ _y

mu_ mu_ _y d_y t_y

Handwriting: entries at the blue line, no entry at the start of a word. **Spelling and vocabulary**: rhyme.

Trace then write the spoonerisms.

picking your nose –

nicking your pose

jelly beans – belly jeans

jumpy puppy – pumpy juppy

trail snacks – snail tracks

eye ball – bye all

TRAIL SNACKS

Handwriting: entries at the blue line, no entry at the start of a word. **Spelling and vocabulary**: rhyme. **Literary elements**: spoonerisms.

A diagonal join goes from an exit kick at the main line up to the next letter.

Trace then write the letter pairs. Remember to use diagonal joins.

Handwriting: diagonal joins to short letters. **Spelling:** common letter pairs.

Diagonal joins

Trace then write the letter pairs.

Remember to use diagonal joins.

mi mu mm my mp mn

ni nn nu ny kr ki kn

ku hy hi hu im in

ir ly li lu lp lm ti

ty tw tu tr ei em en

er ew ee ep ue me ne ke

Self assessment

My diagonal joins are smooth sometimes ☐ often ☐ always ☐.

Handwriting: diagonal joins to short letters and long letters. **Spelling:** common letter pairs.

You don't need to use an entry at the start of a word. You can also leave off entries and hooks in the middle of words if you are not joining the letters.

Trace then write. Use diagonal joins where you need to.

loan lone

main mane

pain pane

pair pear

paw pour

rain rein

raw roar

hear here

Can you pour with your paw?

Handwriting: diagonal joins to short letters. **Grammar:** personal pronoun (you), noun group (your paw). **Punctuation:** question mark. **Spelling and vocabulary:** homophones.

To connect a diagonal join to a tall letter, continue the exit kick all the way up to the top.

Make an exit kick . . . then keep going up . . . to the very top . . . then retrace to make the next letter.

Trace then write the letter pairs. Remember to use diagonal joins.

ik il it ib ub ul ut

uk mb ml nb nh nt

nk nl ab ah at ak al

cl ch ck ct cl el et

Handwriting: diagonal joins to tall letters. **Spelling:** common letter pairs.

Trace then write the letter pairs. Remember to use diagonal joins.

eb th tt tl dt dl

ht hl kl kh ll lt

Trace then write. Use diagonal joins where you need to.

knight night

knit nit

cent sent scent

wait weight

sail sale

meat meet

Did you see the nit knit?

Self assessment

I retraced neatly sometimes ☐ often ☐ always ☐.

Handwriting: diagonal joins to tall letters. **Punctuation:** question mark. **Spelling and vocabulary:** common letter pairs, homophones.

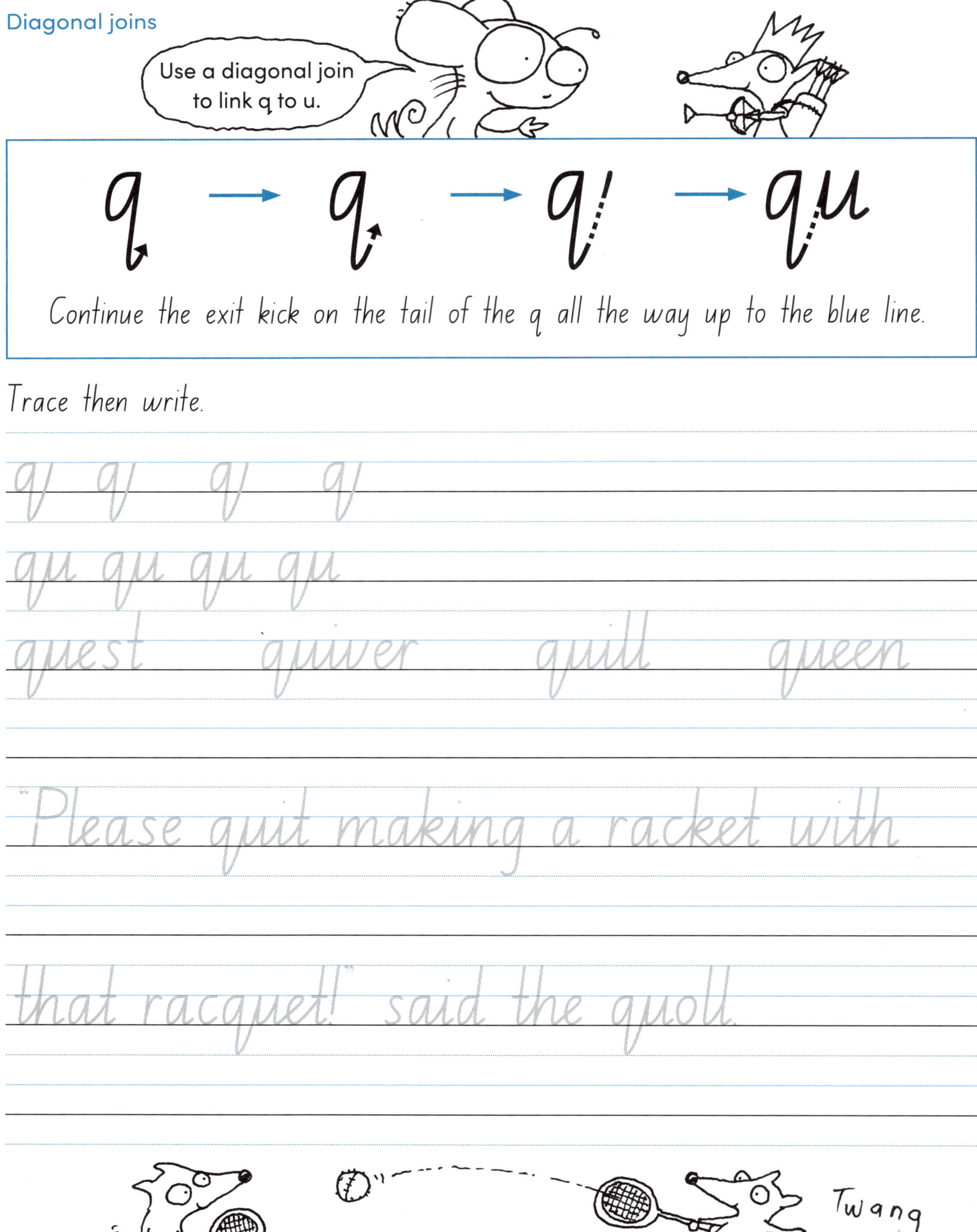

Handwriting: diagonal join q to u. Punctuation: quotation marks, exclamation mark. Spelling and vocabulary: u always follows q, homophones.

To make a diagonal join from the letter z, first make a little wave at the bottom of the z.

z → z → z → zi

Make a little wave . . . then go up to the start of the next letter.

Trace then write. Don't forget to wave at the bottom of each z.

z z z z z z

zi zi zi zi zi zi

ze zi zl zu zy zz ze zi

zip zap zing

sizzle fizzle

lazy crazy hazy

zany zero zillion

Handwriting: diagonal join from z. **Spelling and vocabulary:** rhyme. **Literary elements:** onomatopoeia, alliteration.

Trace then write.

Practise more diagonal joins.

cue queue

days daze

blew blue

quay key

knew new

tail tale

eight ate

maize maze

Write a sentence of your own using one or more of the word pairs.

Self assessment

My diagonal joins are smooth sometimes ☐ often ☐ always ☐.

I retraced neatly sometimes ☐ often ☐ always ☐.

My z's have a little wave at the bottom sometimes ☐ often ☐ always ☐.

Handwriting: diagonal joins revision. **Spelling and vocabulary:** homophones.

The anticlockwise ellipse letters a, c, d, g, o and q are drop-in letters. To join them to a letter that has an exit kick, just drop them in.

Make an exit kick . . . then keep going up, almost to the blue line . . . then lift your pencil and drop-in the letter.

Trace then write. Remember to make a long exit kick and drop-in the second letter.

ua ud ug uc

uq ug iq ko

do ic ha ho

Make sure that the back of the drop-in letter touches the long exit kick.

Trace then write. Put a tick under the drop-in joins.

Handwriting: drop-in joins for anticlockwise ellipse letters a, c, d, g, o, q, after letters with exit kicks. (Drop-in joins at lo, mo, ha, ng in quote.)
Grammar: thinking verb (loved). **Literary elements**: quote from *Charlotte's Web* by EB White (1952).

st p

Trace the letter pairs. Make a long exit kick and drop in the second letter.

id ld la lo id ld

ta ma mo to ma mo

no ng na nd ng nd

Trace then write.

sing thing ring ding

hand stand band grand

hold gold bold sold fold

Handwriting: drop-in joins to anticlockwise ellipse letters a, c, d, g, o, after letters with exit kicks. **Spelling and vocabulary**: common final consonant blends (ng, nd, ld), rhyme.

Add a drop-in letter a, c, d, g, o or q to each word. Then write the word.

m ny
u ly
bla k
di
fud e
slud e
h me
l ve
li uid
bou uet
t ke
m ke
m le
mu dy
son
ban
du k
l ter
m ney
lon

Self assessment

I feel confident about dropping in letters
sometimes ☐ mostly ☐ always ☐.

Handwriting: drop-in joins for anticlockwise ellipse letters a, c, d, g, o, after letters with exit kicks. **Spelling and vocabulary**: 'dge' (fudge, sludge), 'ng' digraph (song, bang, long).

Make sure your drop-in letter touches the exit kick of the letter in front of it.

Trace then write five words for each letter pair. The first one has been done for you.

ud mud thud cloud proud loud

da

do

ha

id

ld

lo

ta

mo

ug

ag

Handwriting: drop-in joins for anticlockwise ellipse letters a, d, o, g, after letters with exit kicks. **Spelling:** common letter pairs.

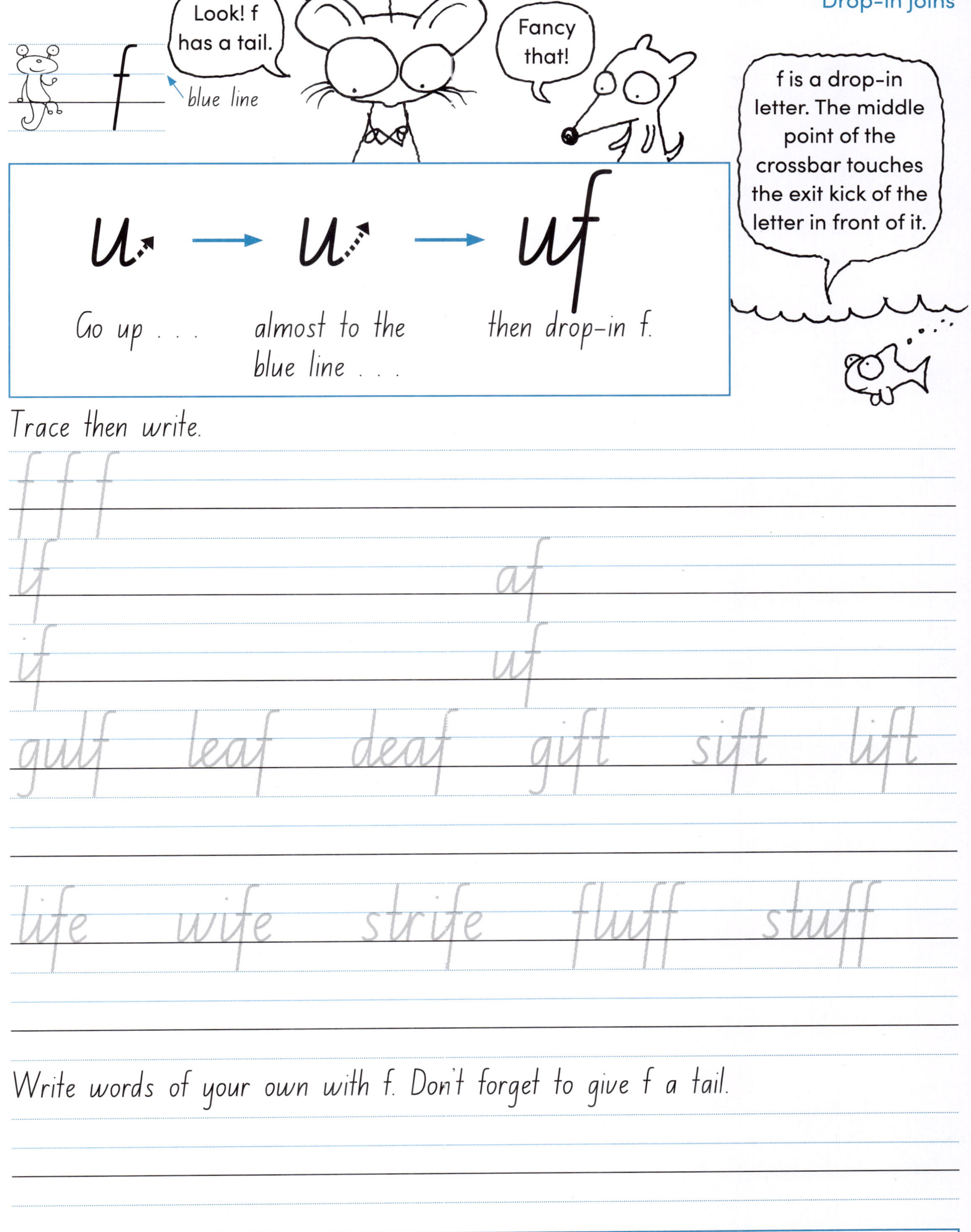

Trace then write.

f f f

if af

if uf

gulf leaf deaf gift sift lift

life wife strife fluff stuff

Write words of your own with f. Don't forget to give f a tail.

Handwriting: drop-in f, f with a tail. **Spelling and vocabulary:** rhyme (gift/sift, fluff/stuff, life/wife).

Join up as much of your writing as you can using all the joins you have learned. Take care with drop-in joins for a, g, c, d, o and f.

Trace then write.

Pinocchio was made of wood.

Pippi Longstocking had red hair.

Mowgli lived in the jungle.

Find some other book character names that use drop-in joins. Write them here in your best writing.

Self assessment

I enjoy writing with joined letters

sometimes ☐ usually ☐ always ☐.

Handwriting: drop-in joins revision. **Grammar**: proper nouns (Pippi Longstocking, Mowgli, Pinocchio). **Punctuation**: capital letters for proper nouns and to start sentences, full stops at the end of sentences. **Literary elements**: references to characters from *Pippi Longstocking* by Astrid Lindgren (1945), *The Jungle Book* by Rudyard Kipling (1894) and *The Adventures of Pinocchio* by Carlo Collodi (1883).

To join from a letter that finishes near the blue line, you need a horizontal join. The letters that finish near the blue line are o, r, v, w and x.

wi vi ry xy

A horizontal join is a line with a little wave.

Trace then write.

vi vu wi wu

oi om ou on

op or ov ow

oz rm ri ru

rr ry rp xi

xu xy wn wy

toy top oil burp

Handwriting: horizontal joins at the blue line, from v, w, o, r, x. **Spelling and vocabulary:** 'oy' digraph (toy), 'oi' digraph (oil), 'ur' digraph (burp).

Horizontal joins

Practise horizontal joins at the blue line from o, r and w.

Trace then write.

SLURP

ow tow show snow below

ow window shadow ri wriggle

ri ripe script wrist ru run

ru rust runny rp burp slurp

rr purr ry furry hurry blurry

Purrr

Handwriting: horizontal joins at the blue line, from w, o, r. **Spelling and vocabulary**: 'ur' digraph (burp), 'ow' digraph (snow), double rr (purr, furry, hurry), silent w (wrist).

Practise horizontal joins.

Trace then write.

oi toil om stomp ou should

on only op open oy boy joy

or short vi vine or story

ow town oz dozen ov oven

oz woozy xi pixie xy xylophone

Handwriting: horizontal joins at the blue line, from v, w, o, r, x. **Spelling and vocabulary**: 'ou' digraph (should), 'oi' digraph (boil, toil), 'or' digraph (pore, short, story), 'oo' digraph (woozy), 'xy' (xylophone, pronounced as *zuy-luh-fohn*), etymology ('phone' from Greek word for sound).

Handwriting: horizontal joins to anticlockwise ellipse letters a, c, d, g, o. **Spelling**: common digraphs 'oo', 'oa'.

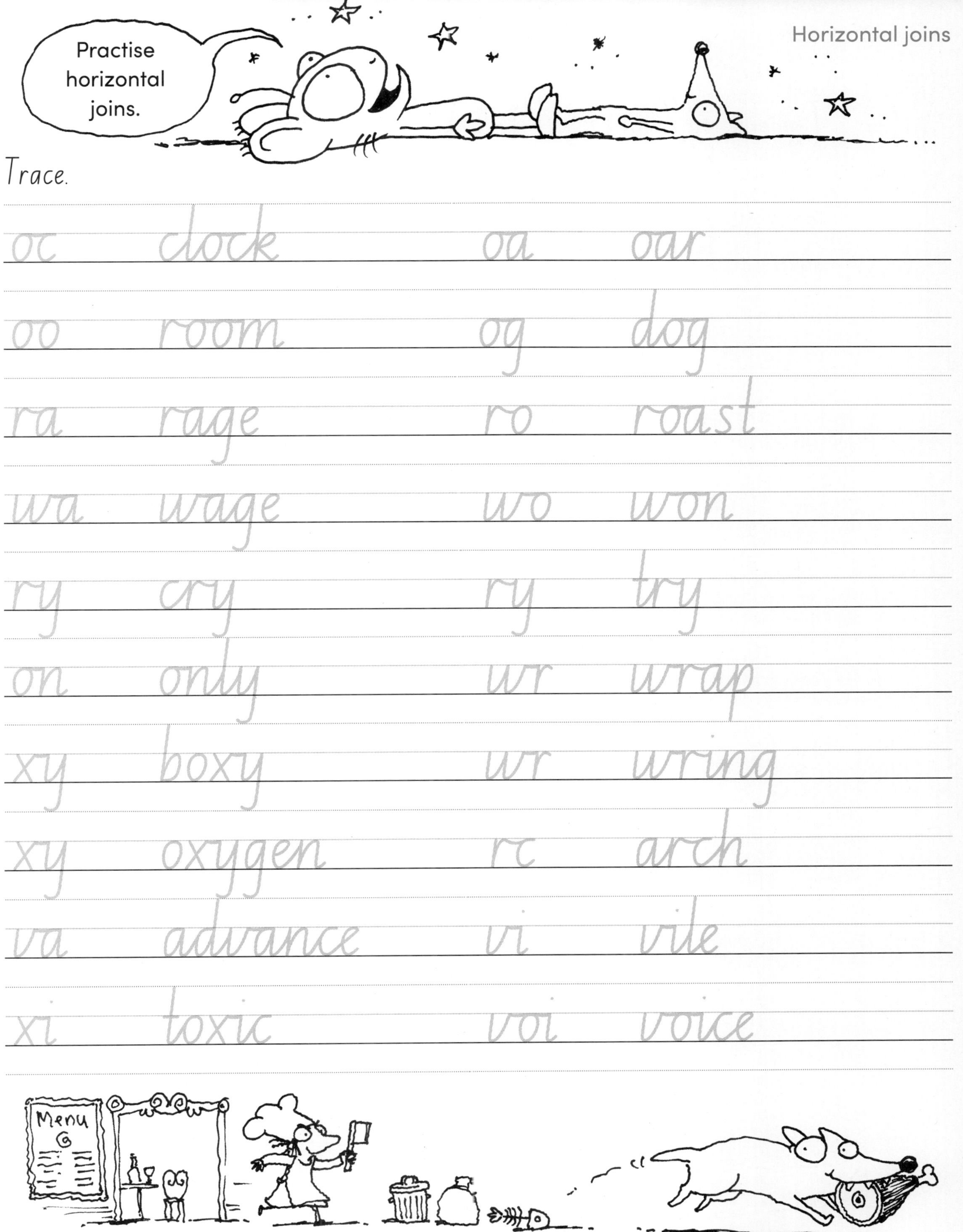

Trace.

oc clock oa oar

oo room og dog

ra rage ro roast

wa wage wo won

ry cry ry try

on only wr wrap

xy boxy wr wring

xy oxygen rc arch

va advance vi vile

xi toxic voi voice

Handwriting: horizontal joins at the blue line and to anticlockwise ellipse letters. **Spelling and vocabulary:** rhyme (wage/rage, cry/try), digraphs 'oo', 'oa', blend 'tr', silent w (wrap, wring).

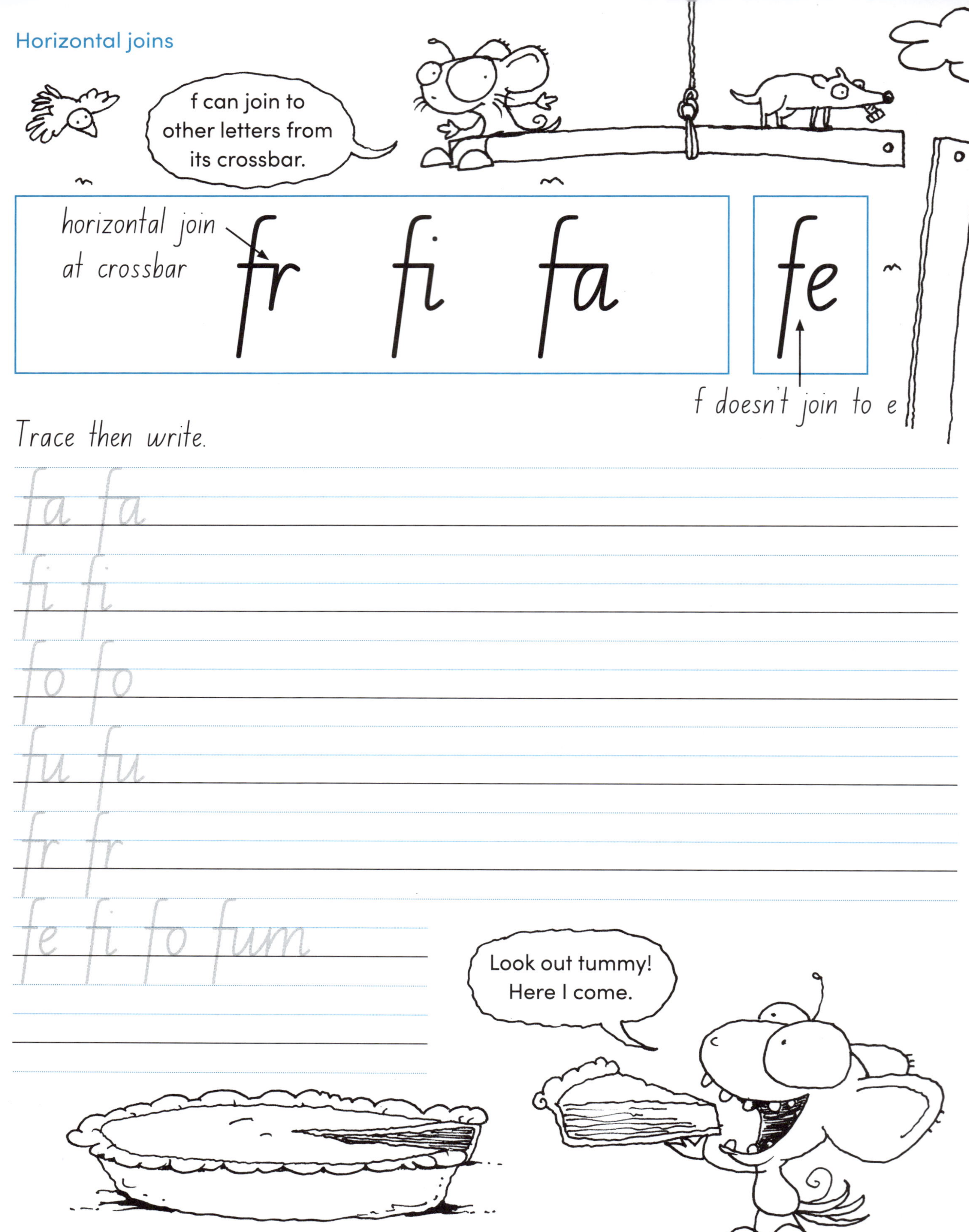

Handwriting: horizontal joins from f, joining f along the crossbar. **Spelling and vocabulary**: rhyme (fum/come). **Literary elements**: reference to folk tale, *Jack and the Beanstalk*.

From the exit . . . go up . . . then retrace down.

Trace then write.

wh who what where which

rl girl curl hurl whirl twirl

rk work rt hurt rf surf turf

My retracing is smooth and neat

rarely ☐ mostly ☐ always ☐.

Handwriting: horizontal joins to tall letters, f, h, k, l, t. **Grammar:** question words/pronouns (who, what, where, which). **Spelling and vocabulary:** 'wh' digraph (who, what, where, which), rhyme (girl/ curl/ hurl/ whirl/ twirl).

Trace then write.

To join the letter o to a tall letter, remember to go up from the blue line and then retrace down.

ot ob oh ol of ok

hot spot slob job gob

oh ooh Pooh Pharaoh

pool cool fool drool off

Pooh's Hunny

book hook cook look took sook

Look. Pooh spells honey funnily.

Handwriting: horizontal join from o to tall letters. **Grammar:** interjections (oh, ooh), proper nouns (Pharaoh, Pooh). **Spelling and vocabulary**: rhyme (book/took, cool/fool, slob/job), 'oo' digraph. **Literary elements**: reference to character (Winnie-the-Pooh) from *When We Were Very Young* by AA Milne (1924).

Practise horizontal joins to tall letters.

Trace then write these words for sounds. Draw a star under the tall letters where you needed to retrace.

whiz whirr growl wham

bawl hoot snarl snort

whack whoosh whoop

woof chortle howl

Write some onomatopoeia words of your own. Tick any horizontal joins where you needed to retrace.

Handwriting: horizontal joins for tall letters. **Spelling and vocabulary**: digraphs 'oo' (whoosh, woof, hoot, whoop), 'aw' (bawl), 'or' (snort, chortle), 'ar' (snarl). **Literary elements**: onomatopoeia.

Horizontal joins

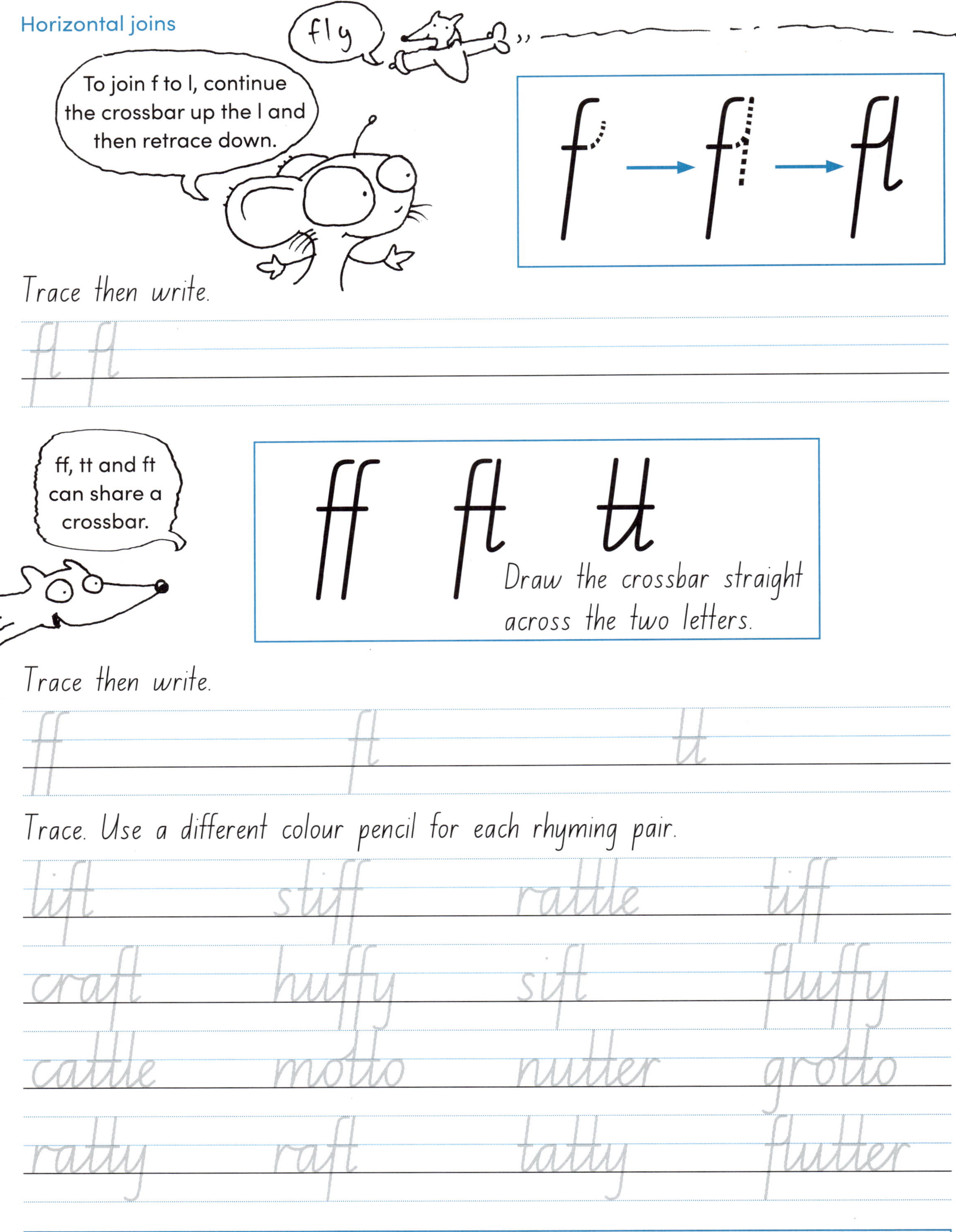

Handwriting: horizontal join from f crossbar, double crossbar. **Spelling and vocabulary**: rhyme, common letter clusters – 'ttle' (cattle).

Trace then write the similes.

as hungry as a wolf

as wary as a fox

as loyal as a dog

surfs like a clown

drools like a hungry monster

as cold as ice

Handwriting: horizontal joins revision. **Literary elements**: similes using 'like' or 'as', reference to folk tale, *Little Red Riding Hood.*

Letters that don't join

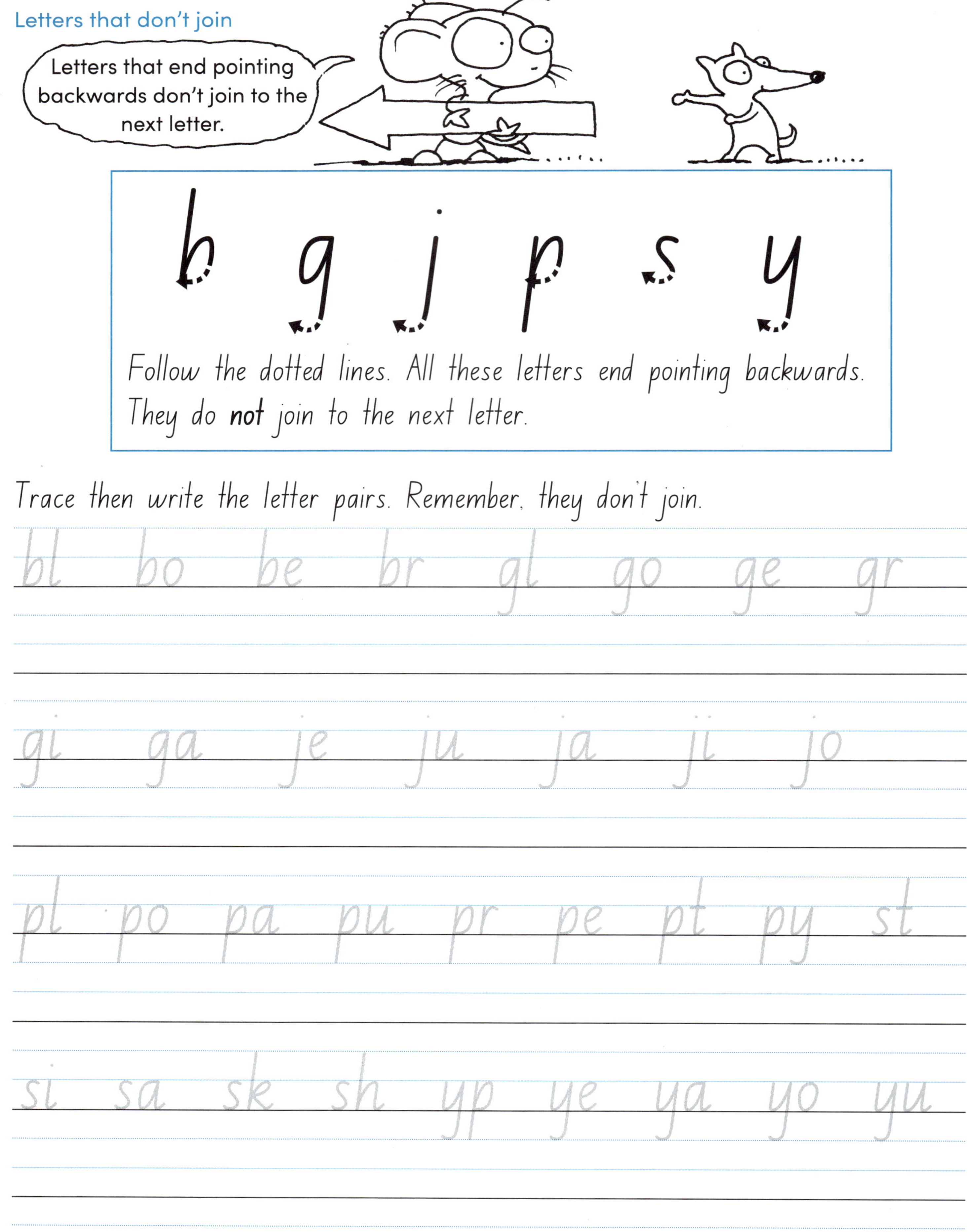

Follow the dotted lines. All these letters end pointing backwards. They do **not** join to the next letter.

Trace then write the letter pairs. Remember, they don't join.

bl bo be br gl go ge gr

gi ga je ju ja ji jo

pl po pa pu pr pe pt py st

si sa sk sh yp ye ya yo yu

Handwriting: letters that don't join. **Spelling:** common letter pairs.

Trace then write. If a letter ends pointing backwards, remember **not** to join it to the next letter.

a gaggle of geese

a band of coyotes

a tribe of goats

a shadow of jaguars

an ambush of tigers

a prickle of porcupines

Make up your own collective nouns.

a of slugs

a of bugs

Self assessment

Others find my handwriting easy to read:

rarely ☐ mostly ☐ always ☐ .

Handwriting: letters that don't join. **Grammar:** collective nouns, articles (a/an). **Spelling and vocabulary:** rhyme (slug/bug).

fe oe re ve we xe

These letters don't join to e.

Trace then write.

a skulk of foxes

a drove of cattle

a shiver of sharks

a business of ferrets

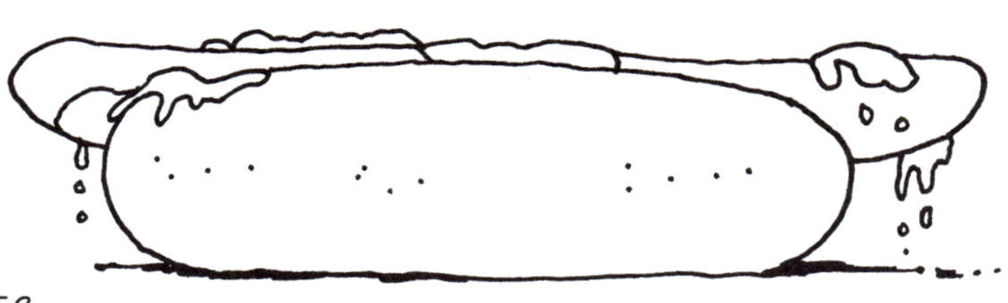

Trace.

I have a very large, hot dog.

I have a very large hot dog.

When I write, my hand and arm are relaxed and comfortable: rarely ☐ mostly ☐ always ☐ .

Handwriting: letters that don't join to e. **Grammar:** collective nouns, comma to separate adjectives in a list. **Punctuation:** comma.

Trace then write.

"Why did you call him Tortoise,

if he wasn't one?" Alice asked.

"We called him Tortoise because he

taught us," said the Mock Turtle

angrily.

Handwriting: practising all joins. **Grammar:** proper nouns (Tortoise, Mock Turtle), pronouns (you, him, he, we, us), compound sentence, conjunction (because), complex sentence with subordinating conjunction (if), adverb (angrily), reference (Tortoise-one). **Punctuation**: quotation marks for dialogue/direct speech, full stop, capital letters for proper nouns. **Spelling and vocabulary**: apostrophe for contraction (wasn't), digraphs 'au' (because, taught), 'or' (tortoise). **Literary elements:** pun/word play (tortoise/taught us), quote from *Alice's Adventures in Wonderland* by Lewis Carroll (1865).

Trace then write. Link each underlined noun group with its meaning on the right.

Look out for a Noah's Ark.

Have a butcher's hook.

What's the John Dory?

Let's hit the frog and toad.

I'll have a dog's eye.

a look

the road

a pie

the story

a shark

Handwriting: practising all joins. **Grammar:** noun groups, proper nouns (Noah's Ark, John Dory), question, possessive apostrophes (Noah's, butcher's, dog's). **Punctuation**: question mark. **Literary elements**: rhyming slang.

This is a quote from a story called *The Tale of Peter Rabbit.*

Trace then write.

Don't go into Mr McGregor's

garden: your Father had

an accident there: he was

put in a pie by Mrs McGregor.

Write a safety warning of your own. It can be a warning for a friend, family member, or story character. It can be sensible or silly.

Handwriting: practising all joins. **Grammar:** warnings (Don't), commands start with a verb or verb group (Do not go), possessive apostrophe (Mr McGregor's), proper noun (McGregor). **Punctuation**: colon, semicolon. **Spelling and vocabulary:** apostrophes for contraction (Don't). **Literary elements**: play on words and understatement (accident/put in a pie), quote from *The Tale of Peter Rabbit* by Beatrix Potter (1902).

This quote is from a story called *The Road to Oz*. Polychrome is the Rainbow's daughter.

Trace then write.

"Haven't you any dewdrops, or

mist-cakes, or cloudbuns?" asked

Polychrome, longingly.

"Course not," replied Dorothy.

Dewdrops, mist-cakes and cloudbuns are food that Polychrome likes to eat. Make up some food words of your own that you think sound delicious.

Handwriting: practising all joins. **Grammar:** question, negative question word (Haven't), adverb (longingly), proper nouns (Polychrome, Dorothy). **Punctuation**: quotation marks, question mark, commas to separate items in a list, full stop, capital letter for proper noun. **Spelling and vocabulary**: Poly meaning many, chrome from Greek 'chroma' meaning colour, apostrophe for contraction (haven't), **Literary elements**: quote from *The Road to Oz* by L Frank Baum (1909), play on food and weather words (dewdrops, mist-cakes, cloudbuns).

Add as many labels as you can think of to the map. Use your best printing.

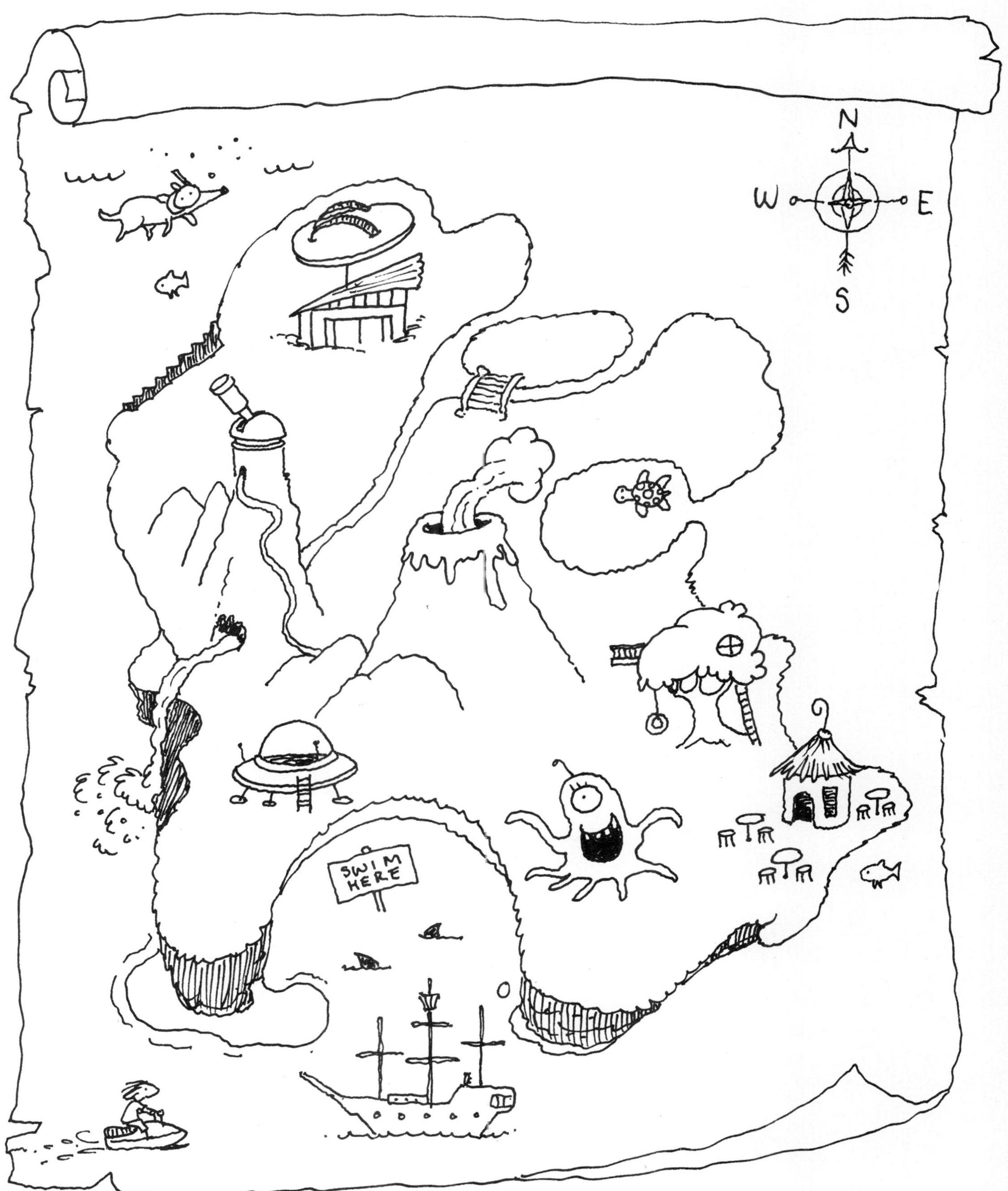

Handwriting: using printing to label maps and diagrams. **Literary elements:** fantasy.

Consolidation

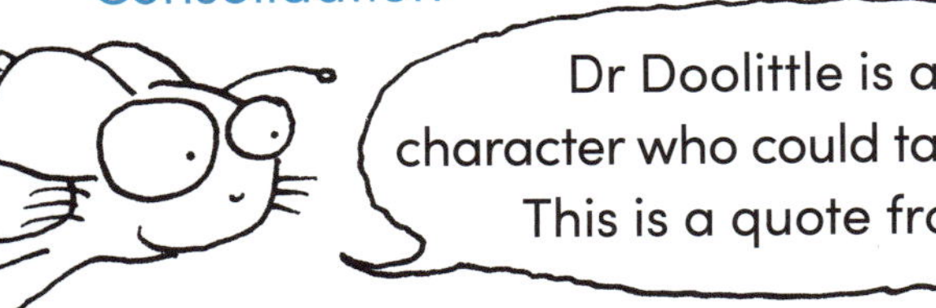

Copy it in your best joined handwriting.

"Oh that," said the Doctor, turning around – "that's a Wiff-Waff. Its full name is hippocampus pippitopitus."

Scientific name: hippocampus pippitopitus

Make up your own creature and give it a scientific sounding name. Draw a picture of it. Label its features.

Remember to use printing for labels.

Handwriting: practising all joins, using printing to label diagrams. **Grammar:** pronouns (that, that's, its), direct/quoted speech. **Punctuation:** quotation marks, comma. **Literary elements**: quote from *The Voyages of Doctor Doolittle* by Hugo Lofting (1922).

Trace the nonsense poem.

JABBERWOCKY by Lewis Carroll

'Twas brillig, and the slithy toves
Did gyre and gimble in the wabe:
All mimsy were the borogoves,
And the mome raths outgrabe.

Here are some more nonsense words. Write a meaning for each one. Then complete the table with some more nonsense words of your own.

Remember to use your best cursive writing.

NONSENSE WORD	PART OF SPEECH	MEANING
snismy	adjective	
groot	verb	
borotroves	noun	

Handwriting: capitals, printing, cursive. **Grammar:** parts of speech. **Punctuation:** apostrophe, comma, colon. **Spelling and vocabulary:** nonsense words, portmanteau words (slithy = lithe and slimy, mimsy = miserable and flimsy). **Literary elements:** poetry (ballad), quote from 'Jabberwocky' from *Through the Looking Glass* by Lewis Carroll (1872).

Consolidation

Write a list of 10 things you'd like to do when you are older. Your ideas can be crazy or serious. It's up to you . . . just as long as you write them in your best joined-up handwriting. Don't forget to number your list 1 to 10.

Ten things to do challenge

Handwriting: practising all joins, numerals 1 to 10.

A comma can make a big difference.

Copy the sentence that labels the picture.

Kenji walked on, his head held high.

Kenji walked on his head, held high.

Trace then write. Then illustrate each sentence.

Let's eat Dad.

Let's eat, Dad.

Handwriting: practising all joins. **Grammar:** pronoun ('us' in Let's). **Punctuation:** comma to separate a phrase.

All was a-shake and a-shiver – glints and gleams and sparkles, rustle and swirl, chatter and bubble.

Assessment 1 – Exits and entries Date ____________

Rewrite the text above using all the entries and exits that you have learned.

Assessment 2 – Diagonal joins Date ____________

Rewrite the text above using all the exits and diagonal joins that you have learned.

Grammar: adjectives, common nouns, action verbs, saying verbs. **Literary elements:** quote from *The Wind in Willows* by Kenneth Grahame (1908).

All was a-shake and a-shiver – glints and gleams and sparkles, rustle and swirl, chatter and bubble.

Assessment 3 – Drop-in joins Date ____________

Rewrite the text above using all the diagonal joins and drop-in joins that you have learned.

Assessment 4 – Horizontal joins Date ____________

Rewrite the text above using your best cursive handwriting.

Grammar: adjectives, common nouns, action verbs, saying verbs. **Literary elements:** quote from *The Wind in Willows* by Kenneth Grahame (1908).

Read each of the criteria listed below. When you think you have achieved each one, write the date and sign off.

Criteria	✓	Date and sign off
My letters are the right shape.	☐	
My letters are a consistent size.	☐	
My letters are a consistent height.	☐	
My letters sit on the main line correctly.	☐	
My letter tails hang down correctly.	☐	
My letters are the same slope.	☐	
The space between my letters is regular.	☐	
The space between my words is regular.	☐	
My joins are smooth.	☐	
I can do all the joins.	☐	
My writing flows.	☐	
I can write quite quickly when I need to.	☐	
Others can easily read my cursive handwriting.	☐	

Have you signed off on each of the criteria for fluent and legible handwriting?
You've successfully completed your handwriting journey.

Congratulations!